Praise for *Raw Wounds*

"*Raw Wounds* is an explosive indictment on injustice. Kondwani Fidel's passion bleeds through the pages. His voice is timely, energetic, youthful, powerful, and fearless."—**MK Asante, bestselling author of *Buck: A Memoir***

"Kondwani Fidel is gem––a gem that shines so bright, it's even visible in the darkest of places. And from those dark places comes *Raw Wounds*, a story that clearly documents the many layers of Blackness in a way that only a person with his lived experience can. *Raw Wounds* is eye-opening to outsiders and liberating to those who lived and are still living these experiences. Fidel has a literary gift and we are fortunate that he chose to share it with us. *Raw Wounds* is brilliant and I highly recommend it to anybody in search of the truth."—**D. Watkins, New York Times bestselling author of *The Beast Side and The Cook Up***

"Kondwani's work is honest and imaginative, pushing us to confront our realities while reminding us of the hope we need to endure. He is an artist who understands his role as an activist, using language to empower, to enrich, and to inform." —**DeRay McKesson, civil rights activist**

"Kondwani has a unique way of connecting with all people. This book is real, raw, and necessary." —**Torrey Smith, NFL Player**

"*Raw Wounds* is an essential report from the ground of America's most overlooked and vilified territory. Kondwani Fidel brings the smell, taste, and sounds of the day-to-day life that many Black Americans experience, effectively humanizing those who are too often othered as a means to erase."
—**Lawrence Burney, *Noisey***

"This book reveals the importance of decision-making and knowing your history. Being an athlete is one way to get out of poverty, but demonstrating leadership through literacy is another." —**Charles Tapper, NFL Player**

"As poet Kondwani Fidel compartmentalizes his thoughts dealing with national and local issues, he supports each story, each memory, each moment of introspection with poignant lines. Kondwani uses vivid imagery to cast the reader right in the middle of each scene and writes from a place of truth and vulnerability." —**Reginald C. Thomas II,** *City Paper*

"Kondwani Fidel's talent is the bonafide voice of our collective future." —**Glenn Singleton, founder of** *The Pacific Educational Group*

"Not everyone knows the perils of poverty, of the concrete roses that are drizzled with soot. Not everyone has seen real life dope fiends, nodding on unswept stoops. Not everyone has to walk past boarded buildings as a requirement to get to their home. Not everyone knows what it feels like to really celebrate seeing your 21st birthday, not because you are "legal," but because you thought you'd never make it. But, most importantly, not everyone knows what it means to be that big brother who made it beyond the tender young years that society established for his death, reached dreams that were once unimaginable, and now must strive to guide a younger brother who is not yet there. Not everyone feels and sees the preserved mental images of death, that "lone sneaker" that always ends up over there after a person loses their life to gun violence. Not every work provides that vivid image for those who do not live these experiences. *Raw Wounds* invokes such powerful and tangible memories for those who share the same struggle, and are thus able to see, feel, smell, hear, and taste what's presented.

Beautiful Kondwani Fidel has once again composed a masterpiece of stories and memories that forms lessons to all young Suns growing up in the neighborhood.

This piece, this lesson, is ever so necessary in an era where, we, who come from urban communities, are still fighting structural racism, police bru-

tality, economic genocide while simultaneously fighting the ways in which we self-destruct, destroy one another, and create chaos in our communities. It is a critique of the system of our oppression and a critique of the dysfunctions in our own families, relationships, and communities. It is brilliant that a young mind such as Fidel's has been blessed with the conscious and creative spirit that allows him to compose a lesson from a perspective and in a way that no other could. *Raw Wounds* is sung in pitches and frequencies that invokes the emotion. It is a bittersweet song."
—Dr. Zoe Spencer, Associate Professor in the Department of Sociology and Criminal Justice at Virginia State University

RAW WOUNDS

KONDWANI FIDEL

Cover Design & Illustration by Mikea Hugley
@mikeahugley
www.mikeahugley.com

Photos by Reginald C. Thomas, II

Author: Kondwani Fidel

Title: Raw Wounds

Dog Hungry Entertainment, LLC
KondwaniFidel.com

"Oh, I had so many days of crying
Oh, I had so many days of pain
Have you ever been as sad as I am?
Lord, I ask if anything will change?
I can see the future that we're heading
I would say it's better not to tell
If it's anything like this in Heaven
Maybe I'd be better off in Hell."
— J. Cole

"I'm 23 years old. I might just be my mother's child, but in reality, I'm everybody's child. Nobody raised me; I was raised in this society."

— Tupac Shakur

A song for my little brother

Contents

Introduction

The sky is a raw wound, dripping red blood. The sky is a bunch of London buses. The sky is an uncooked steak. The sky is a broken brick home. The sky is on fire and you can't put it out. My sky is not blue. The scant brown grass that peeks through the concrete is scared of a new life. Why? Because people crucify your accomplishments in the disguise of judging the sins that your father dropped on your back. They always overlook those roses that stretch through the concrete. The streets are a heavenly body. A body that you can only fully understand if you trace your finger between every crevice on every part.

My tongue is coated with the truth. My truth. I'm naked, and enjoying every bit of it. Enjoy your nakedness before it's too late. Before someone comes tapping on the door, telling you to "hurry up." So you rush, scrambled and lost in your nakedness, opposed to painting the town in it.

You can't stay in the bathroom forever. So while you are there, show your naked ass. Shout until your lungs collapse because they are going to stop working anyway. Dance until your toes crumble, because they're going to stop moving one day. Death is just like life, they both come at you fast. Both are fastballs, waiting to strike away your nakedness. Enjoy your nakedness before you strike out. Enjoy your nakedness before it's too late.

Your generation, along with the abilities that you all possess, have been stifled by America's racism. There is a lack of faith in Black people, but especially young Black people. I say that because I hear more than often, the term, "this generation," followed by torment. I wouldn't be a man, let alone a big brother, if I allowed these false accusations about you and your generation to flourish without giving the world any static.

Some people will blame you for having drug addicted parents, or no parents. For being forced to receive education in a broken school system. For living amongst prostitutes, fiends, guns, drugs, and liquor stores. People will blame you, opposed to blaming the environment, or whoever created the environment, that chains you.

That ideology is the same of people who support rape. After a skirt is forced off, panties are ripped from the skin, and that woman is raped, there will be some who say, "Why was she wearing that?" or "Do you think he would rape her?" or "She wouldn't have gotten raped if she wasn't being a freak." Blaming the rape victim instead of the rapist. Just how some people will blame the Black struggle in America on Black people, and not the racist ideas and polices that have and continue to enslave, murder, and oppress Black people.

Expressing the truths about America, our family, and my own vulnerabilities is what made this letter very special to me, and hopefully special to you. I hope that anyone who picks up this book will understand the combat of being Black in America through my eyes. I believe that all people of all different groups should dwell together in unity. However, this will only happen if we all see and treat one another as human beings.

It was early in the morning. The sun was slowly climbing.

I woke up out of my sleep to a rambunctious BANG, which was followed by rapid footsteps.

It was you running through the front door playing with your friends.

No, we were getting robbed.

No, it was a gang of pigs.

My mind began to do gymnastics. All I kept thinking about was you; wondering which one of your crimes led them here.

Wondering whose house you broke into.

Wondering whose grandson you greeted with a pistol along with the phrase, "Kick that shit out!" A mundane phrase you hear while growing up in Baltimore.

Wondering whose Dodge minivan you've claimed as your own.

My mind still doing black flips. Just wondering. Why am I even here?

Boots and black door knockers slammed through every door in our home. The same boots that have been smashing the spinal cords, voice boxes, and opportunities of Black people for decades. That knocker that has a rainbow on the front of it because of the mob of doors it has kissed.

"Everyone get the fuck down!" squawked out of every pair of thin pasty lips. Flashlights and pistols waved like a parade. I've had encounters with police officers too many times in my life; some due to my misunderstood childhood habits, and some that were destined because of the long curse of the enslavement of Black people. Either way, I've seen more cops than I've wanted to.

Two of the officers slung me out of my room, almost detaching a shoulder from the rest of my skeleton. They slammed me to the faded brown chipped wooden floor that splintered my face. I was a piece of property to them. I hear a female voice: "What are y'all arresting him for?"

The officer who was built like Bowser from Mario Brothers bulldozed his knee on the back of my hairline, while another one slapped me in handcuffs, chopping my blood circulation, then dragging me across the floor by my arm. My chest was erupting in flames. "I might be the next Freddie Gray," I said to myself. For a million moons we have witnessed police officers drain the blood out of unarmed Black people. We saw the inhumane tactics that were inflicted upon Tamir Rice, Eric Garner, Alton Sterling, and the others. The list goes on. The list will continue to go on.

Still partially asleep, I began to remember Grandma is in the room adjacent to mine. I yelled, "Grandma, just do what they say!" I only said that foolishness because my sleepiness was getting the best of me. My words couldn't save Grandma from racist killer cops. Nothing can save you from them. Not Black or white Jesus. She could've easily been the next Kathryn Johnston, the 92-year-old woman in Atlanta who was murdered in her home by undercover police in a botched drug raid. I've heard too many stories where officers came through front doors, guns blazing, tearing apart the flesh of the innocent.

BANG. A shot fired.

My heart became a clenched fist. Embittered and filled with anxiety, I asked myself, "Will my twisted face flood the media, while my eyes cradle tears, telling the world about America and how unfair she is?"

Grandma, another Black innocent woman gunned down by a Baltimore City cop.

Broken Heirlooms

I remember vividly, I was sitting on the living room floor playing Donkey Kong on my Gameboy Color, while eating a slice of pizza. Grandma was sitting in her single woman chair, glasses sealed to her face, eyes glued to The Baltimore Sun, with a Newport living on the corner of her mouth.

"Shit, did you see that?"

"See what?"

"We got anotha' mouse in here!"

My eyeballs scanned the room for a rodent, but I didn't see it. Mice in the hood can probably outrun any track star you can think of. I wasn't worried about no damn mouse so I finished crushing my pizza and playing my game. Grandma came over to me and snatched my Gameboy from out of my hand. "C'mon! You gotta go to John's Bargains to get some sticky pads. I'm tired of these lil fuckers."

"Okay," I responded in the most bothered way possible. I got up. "What kind do you want me to get?"

"I dunno, just get the good kind," Grandma said.

Grandmothers love "the good kind" of anything. All they wanna know is if this "good kind" is worth their money. I grabbed my dusty black leather jacket, laced up my Nike boots, and made my way to John's Bargains. John's Bargains is one of those spots that sell everything from clothes, to cigarette products, to movies, to books, and I even think you could file your taxes there. On my journey to JB, I saw nodding fiends, young teens playing tackle football on the concrete, and I heard kids cursing more than Bernie Mac.

"Your mother is an ugly bitch."

"Give me back my damn ball."

"Leave me alone dummy."

"Don't make me slap the shit outta you."

"That's why I did it to your sister."

A bunch of kids who probably haven't seen a vagina since they came out of one. A few of the festivities in Baltimore that adds to its bittersweetness.

I got to the store, purchased "the good kind" of sticky pads, then I bounced. When I returned home, I opened several pads and laid them in the main corners that mice typically ran. Grandma rewarded me for performing this task by allowing me to keep the change from the $20 bill that I used to buy the pads.

The next day I was awakened by a ruffling noise that slithered from the bathroom. I went to go check it out, and it was the mouse. Trapped! I have never been the best when it came to playing sports, but the touchdown dance that I enacted was far beyond the greatest dance you've probably ever seen. Grandma was just as happy, and looked as if she wanted to bust a move with me. But instead, she burned her cigarette and cracked a perky smile.

"Glad we caught that little bitch. Now go throw it away," she told me.

Grandma didn't know that I was scared of mice, so picking up a live and breathing mouse was never in my plans, ever in life. Even today. So don't ask. If God whispered in my ear and said, "My child, I need you to pick up the mouse." I would've replied, "Sorry God, you're the one with the powers. How about you pick it up?"

I convinced her to leave it there and wait for it to die, and then I'd throw it away. She agreed. We both went our separate ways for the day.

A few hours later, I heard Grandma yell, "Ain't this some shit?"

I ran upstairs and asked her what was wrong.

She replied, "The damn mouse got away."

I ran in the bathroom and she was right; the mouse had vanished, leaving nothing behind but a few turds and some grey fur that got ripped off by the glue.

I looked at Granny and said, "I don't know how it got away. I guess the good kind aren't as good as you thought."

She smacked the living shit out of my lips, causing them to slightly bleed. I stood there, pitiful, dabbing my index finger on my bottom lip, staring at the blood. I wanted to say, "Hey shorty, don't ever hit me again before I get my other grandmother to whip yo' ass." But I didn't say that because I knew I would've been shedding blood by the bucket.

She snatched my hand and said, "Stop touching your damn lip before I smack you again. Your ass shoulda threw the mouse away when I asked. You never do what I ask you to do."

The pitiful look on my face grew. I shrugged and went back to my room. I was confused as to why Grandma was so upset about the mouse getting away. She was angrier than Kanye. I kept saying to myself, "It's only a mouse."

Later on in life, I figured out why Grandma was so upset. She spent money and faith on a sticky pad, which is a trap designed for the capture and destruction of a rodent. The mouse that we caught was supposed to stay trapped and later die. It didn't.

In this situation, Grandma is a representation of the oppression in America. We, as in Black people, are the mice. This particular mouse that Grandma was upset with is the Black person in America who rises above society's expectations. When he or she receives a high school diploma in a dilapidated school system. Read on and above grade level in a system that tries to keep us underwater. Staying out of prison in a country that's designed for us to live there. Receiving college degrees. Nurturing our children and teaching them the truth about their history. Living past 21 years old. These are a few things that enrage the racists in this society.

We have the ability to thrive in this country despite the ill-boding obstacles we face. I believe that one of the first obstacles is understanding that at birth, Black people in this country are driven to exist in the most horrific areas of this country. Once you understand that, then I believe that you will have a better chance at winning in this game of life.

America is a sticky pad for Black people and people of color, mainly the ones who live in poverty. I want you to escape the trap.

This mouse and trap lesson isn't the only thing that I've learned from Grandma.

Following my birth, on June 3, 1993, Grandma took a moral obligation to adopt me with hopes of creating a cutting edge lane for the betterment of my future. She quit her job working at Signet Bank, and received her license to become a day care provider: all a part of her master plan to raise a young Black man in one of America's deadliest cities. Grandma isn't and never has been one of those holy or spiritual people; however, her heart is auriferous.

She put me in a private Catholic elementary school because she believed that private institutions were "better" than city schools. I never understood the whole religion thing while in school. Mass before class every Wednesday. It felt like a funeral. Annoying hymns and songs that I couldn't comprehend. Every Mass service, I scratched my head and wondered why Catholics drank out of the same gold cup during communion. I wasn't entitled to drink because I was not a part of the Catholic faith. It honestly was a blessing because I thought it was weird for all of those strangers to drink out of the same cup. I thought it was disgusting.

Every day after school, Grandma made sure that I came home and sat at the dining room table and completed all of my homework before I got involved in any other activities. At bedtime, she read me books, many that were written by Dr. Seuss. My favorite was *Are You My Mother?* which is a story about a mother abandoning her unhatched egg. While the mother was gone, the egg hatched, and the baby bird did not understand why his mother left him. He started searching for his mother and the bird lost its ability to fly. I read this book with Grandma for a great deal of days. Every time I read it, I felt like the abandoned bird in the book. Wondering why Mother left me. Searching for her existence and love. In the process, I began to lose my ability to fly, which plunged me into the arcane pit of the streets. I don't think that Grandma knew the importance of reading, but she knew that reading to your child was the "right thing to do." Despite all of this reading I did as a child, I didn't fully understand the importance of reading until several years later, my freshman year at Virginia State University.

Grandma always taught me how I should treat women. "I don't care what a woman does. You never put your hand on one. You get anotha female to whip her ass if you have to. But keep your damn hands to yourself," she would always tell me. I remember in the fourth grade, a girl told the teacher that I hit her, when in all actuality, I didn't; I blocked her from hitting me and she hurt herself. My teacher reported that incident to Grandma, and I got an ass whipping for seven days straight.

Another thing, Grandma always preached about how bad homosexuality was. "You know it's a lot of faggots out there in the world now. If you ever feel like you wanna play with a dick you better play with your own." Being gay seemed as if it was a disease and Grandma wasn't the only person who felt this way. I never fully understood Grandma's anger towards "faggots" because she had a friend who was a "faggot." His name was Mr. Ron. He'd come around from time to time and drink canned Budweisers with Grandma and they would get pissy drunk while gossiping and having "girl talk." I never said a word about it though. Even though I wanted to say, "Hey, Grandma! Why you tell me not to be a faggot when Mr. Ron is a faggot?" But I didn't say anything because I know she probably would've kicked me in my damn mouth.

Aunt Sharice was the same way: confused about whether she hated "faggots" or not because she too had a friend, Mr. Charlie, who was one. Mr. Charlie and Mr. Ron both popped their chewing gum like uzis, shook their bodies like engines as they strutted like runway models, and talked with expansive lisps, their tongues hanging out of their mouths how winos hang outside of bars.

There was one specific church visit that made me question my aunt views on "faggots."

During a sermon, the pastor was talking about "faggtos" going to Hell because it was a sin for men to sleep with other men and for women to sleep with other women. Aunt Sharice was tossing her chin up and down, saying, "Yes pastor! You go pastor! I know that's right pastor!" I sat beside her, confused. Her best friend was a "faggot." I wanted to take my hand and smack her lips and say, "Aunt Sharice. You should be ashamed of yourself. Throwing shade at Mr. Charlie. He's been a good "faggot" to you all this time and you go behind his back." But I didn't say that because she probably would've killed me right there in that church pew. Leaving blood on every nearby Bible and bystander.

As I got older, I learned that my aunt, along with many other churchy people, tend to hide their sins and false judgements behind smiles, offerings, and Sunday worship. I got older and realized that the same pastor who condemned "faggots" turned out to like men himself—young boys to be exact. When I became older, I also learned that my aunt wasn't the holiest person either, due to the abundance of sins she was committing. As I got older I also realized that the term "faggot" was derogatory, and I stripped it off of my tongue.

I remember Oprah interviewing Dave Chapelle in 2006. Dave said, "The hardest thing to do is to be true to yourself, especially when everyone is watching." I took heed to that quote, and decided that I would never be a fake in order to make someone else comfortable, even if those persons are "churchy," or family. Mr. Ron or Mr. Charlie didn't give a damn about anyone's thoughts pertaining to their "lifestyle" because they were openly being who they wanted to be in a world that condemns people like them to Hell. Growing up, I've seen gay guys get stomped out and beaten with metal bats until their teeth scattered onto the ground. So a sin or not, Mr. Ron and Mr. Charlie were some brave guys when I look back.

I mention this because I want people to understand that they are not free until they fully accept themselves. If a person judges another due to their "lifestyle," that speaks volumes on the judger's character. Everyone is expeditious when it comes to judging someone else, but never check their own underwear for shit stains.

I don't believe that a sexual orientation is an automatic Hell sentence, nor do I believe that a sexual preference determines what you can contribute to your people. Too many times, I hear people devalue others' revolutionary, spiritual, and community services because of their sexuality or gender. If we all honored who we are, then we would have the fullest of freedom because collectively as a people we will be liberated.

Out of all the things Grandma taught me, the biggest lesson was to never become anyone's crutch because they will use you for their own personal gain until your death bed. She didn't verbally tell me this; however, I learned it through actions, and how she allowed herself to be mistreated, abused, physically and mentally, by her daughter: our mother. I can't count how many times I've heard our mother call Grandma "a dirty bitch" and threatened to kill her. I can't erase the permanent memories of my Christmas toys being stolen by her. Several days throughout my childhood she would harass me and Grandma in the middle of Monument Street while we were trying to go grocery shopping at Maury's Steakhouse and Northeast Market. I can't shake the nightmares of my peers and family members telling me, "Your mother is a trifling junkie bitch" whenever we got involved in petty arguments, which drove me to heartache, tears, and sometimes fistfights. These are not even a quarter of the troubles I faced growing up, but these troubles taught me not to ever let someone take advantage of you repeatedly because it will cause destruction on you and the people around you. Grandma is still reaping the obstruction from the results of being someone's lifelong crutch. Since childhood, I've seen Grandma inhale trucks of cigarettes and gallons of alcohol. Despite her addictions, if she died today, I bet her autopsy would read "stress."

* * *

Knocks came hitting my door like bullets. It was a Saturday afternoon. It was my father. I ran to the door to let him in, and he stood there on my steps with his curly hair, pumpkin sized nose, and his contagious smile.

"What's up?" he said.

He always had a devilish sort of grin on his face. But in that same grin, if you stared hard enough, you would fall in love because you saw value. One of those smiles you will remember for a lifetime.

"Nothing much," I said.

"Yo have you seen Tim?" he asked me. Tim was a friend of mine. We'd been friends forever. We used to lend each other clothes, money, and we use to slang heroin together. I was a little confused why my father was at my peep-hole, asking for Tim, at 8:30 in the morning. However, I pointed. "He's right up there on Jefferson and Milton," which was two blocks up from my home.

My father said, "Okay," and I watched him skirt off in a blue Dodge minivan. I went back in the crib and went to go pour me some Cinnamon Toast Crunch. I devoured the bowl, reached for the box and poured more, then my phone rang. I sprinted upstairs. Tim was calling me. I picked up. "Yo what's good?"

"Yo you won't believe this shit."

"What happened yo?"

"Ya father just fuckin robbed me yo."

An awkward silence pinched both ends of the phone. Lost for words, I said, "Damn, foreal?" In hindsight, I don't believe that statement was good for that moment.

"What the fuck do you mean foreal?' I know what your father look like."

We spent the next few minutes arguing with each other. The conversation ended with Tim saying, "Fuck you yo. You're a fraud ass nigga," followed by the dial tone. I sat at the table and watched my Cinnamon Toast Crunch rotate into a soggy sensation.

I felt bad because I had told my father where Tim was. Never in a million years did I think my father would use me as an accomplice to a robbery that involved sticking up one of my friends. This haunted me for years because from then on out, I never knew what my father was capable of. I heard through reliable sources that jamming pistols to the back of people's throats and robbing were habits of his. Also, this wasn't the last time that my father was involved in a robbery dealing with my peers. His malevolent habits could have resulted in my kidnapping or death. In the hood, when someone can't get to an individual, they will attack the closest thing to him or her. And everyone knew that me and my father had an unbreakable love.

I remember in 2008, two teenage brothers that I knew from around East Baltimore were kidnapped and held for ransom. The word on the street was that they got kidnapped for something their older brother, a kingpin, did.

My father has been in and out of prison and jails ever since my first swallow of Gerber Baby. He bamboozled my friends. I've seen him punch dudes in the jaw for cursing in front of me. I still cringe when images of him pop in my head of him nodding, high off heroin. Back then I didn't know that he was on drugs, but whenever I caught him nodding he'd say that it was because of working long hours. His mile long history of lying makes me believe that he didn't really have a job. But in reality, smacking people with pistols, selling drugs, doing drugs, and robbing people, all while you're ducking cops, probably did make a man tired. I constantly hear his voice: "Your mother is a junkie bitch. You don't have to respect her. You only have to respect your grandmother." This played a major role in my hate for Mommy because I listened to a great deal of what my father instilled in me. I never disrespected her, but I grew to hate her. I wish I could say, "I grew to love her less," but I can't.

My father may have been a negative force in my life, however, his positive influence was vital in my process of becoming a man. My father taught me how to fight. He taught me about the wickedness in the streets and how to maneuver through them. He taught me the proper way to stab someone if I was getting jumped. He gave me a silver plated pocket knife and told me to carry it at all times because "These niggas in Baltimore is crazy." He taught me how to dress. His favorite slogan was "It's not about what you wear, but how you wear it," which got me far in life with hooking up with girls. Guys were spending hundreds and sometimes thousands of dollars on clothes and shoes to impress women, and I was hooking up with the same ones in an outfit that cost maybe $200 total, including my socks and boxer-briefs. If I asked my father for money, he'd give me his last, and if he didn't have it on him, he'd find a way to get it for me. When he was around, he encouraged me to get good grades in school. No matter how many drugs my father sold or sniffed, he never put them in my hand and always told me that he didn't want me to follow in his footsteps. He always told me to respect Grandma no matter what. He taught me about the corny dudes in life who will try to act tough but are really timid and weak on the inside. He told me, "People are gonna hate on you when you get older because you're smart, handsome, and slick." My father taught me how to be a man and taught me survival skills that were much-needed growing up in East Baltimore. These things my pops taught me, both positive and negative, have greatly influenced my life. All of the negative things I heard and saw showed me what not to do, while the positive things showed me what to do. Words can be mighty, but actions pack more punches. While growing up, I still did some things that my father told me not to do because he did them. And I wanted to be like him.

I went to visit my father a few weeks ago in prison, where he's been for the past nine years. I remember him saying, "This life that I'm living, these obstacles that I'm going through, is all in God's plan." I don't know if I fully agree with that statement, however, the life that he's lived has played a key role in making me who I am today. Throughout all of this triumph and victory of a boy to a "man," I still mourn. I have a little boy trapped inside of me, who has a little boy trapped inside of him. This little boy still cries for a father. This little boy still cries for a mother. Grandma tried her best, but nothing can fill the void created by lost and disoriented parents.

* * *

Mommy and my father are true examples of those mice that got trapped on the sticky pad. For many years in America, we have blamed Black people for their mishaps instead of blaming the racist policies and ideas that have enslaved, murdered, and oppressed many Black people.

With my own eyes, I have seen the drug epidemic and the lack of resources and opportunities tear a Black family apart. This epidemic still gnaws away at our home and many other homes in impoverished communities. It's impossible for you to have grown up in Baltimore and have not been affected by the drug epidemic. In some households in our city, everyone who lived under the roof consumed crack and heroin, from the grandparents to their children down to the grandchildren. I knew some people that didn't have parents on drugs, but they had an aunt, uncle, cousin, brother, or sister who were crack and heroin addicts. Some people didn't have family that used drugs, but had a friend or a significant other on drugs. Not a friend or significant other? I'm pretty sure they had a friend or significant other who had a friend or a significant other on drugs, or someone in their circle who could relate to the horrific stories related to crack and heroin abuse.

I had a friend named Tony. Tony's dad was robbed and murdered in his driveway. Later, they found the culprit: a junkie had committed that robbery and murder to get money for drugs. I've heard several stories of junkies "being down bad" or "illin." When a fiend is "down bad" or "illin," it means that they don't have any drugs or money to buy drugs, so they end up in a severe state of desperation. During this state of desperation, a junkie who is "down bad" will do anything to get high, even if it involves blowing an infant's brains out for $10. Your occupation, annual income, the size of your rims, your degree, high school diploma, or religion didn't matter. Somehow some way, everybody that I know in Baltimore City was affected by the crack and heroin epidemic.

The lessons I learned from the three of my parents made me who I am today. Grandma didn't have the same energy and patience while raising you in her late 60s and 70s that she had raising me in her 50s and early 60s. I believe that plagues and diseases, when not treated, get worse. Therefore, the damage that our mother did to you while you were under Grandma's supervision was probably worse than what she did during my upbringing.

Being a writer and poet exposed me to the world beyond our own little world in Baltimore. The issues that we face here is merely a symptom of the greater issue in America, which I will later touch on. This world stretches far beyond the liquor stores, junkies, drugs, guns, and prostitutes that we live amongst. This world is suffering tremendously. Due to the oppression of Black people in this country, we don't have any beneficial family heirlooms or legacies that we can follow. From the womb to the world, we have been labeled as monsters. That's why it is up to us to recreate ourselves, and break loose of the image that we are born with. I believe that this will minimize the mental and physical destruction of Black people in this country.

Don't try to be anyone or try not to be anyone. Create you. Find your own answers by reading and gaining intellect. Once you come to a better understanding of who you want to be, then you can free yourself. Then you can help free not only other Black and Brown minorities in this country, but anyone in this world who needs freedom. I believe this is the most impactful legacy anyone could leave behind: a legacy that enriches the development of people in the struggle.

THE RAID

PART.2

BANG! Another shot fired into Grandma's torso.

No, Grandma had a heart attack and collapsed like buckling knees on babies attempting their first walk.

No, it was the cops wreaking havoc in our home.

They split more doors, damaged floors, cracked open boxes of Cinnamon Toast Crunch, assorted flavors of oatmeal (the good kind), spilled it all over the kitchen, dumped trash out of the plastic bags that hung on door knobs, slung clothes everywhere, broke dressers, plastered holes in our walls, broke more doors, and spit tobacco on the floor. The cops' pandemonium reached a crescendo. Their appetite for destruction was carnivorous. I didn't expect any other behavior.

The pigs then guided my half-naked, bony body down the steps, and took me on what seemed to be the longest walk of my life. They smashed me down on the living couch right beside you. Every second I was embracing an early death. I stared at you with a face like a devil sick of sin, and you pathetically lowered your head. If I weren't in cuffs at that moment, I would've gave you the worst ass whipping you ever received in your life.

"What the fuck is wrong with you?" I asked.

"What you talkin' bout?"

"Do you not see what the fuck you puttin Grandma through?"

The officers stared at us while we squabbled, with their hands glued to their guns, looking as if they wanted to silence our bickering with a few bullets.

The room went silent while eye balls struck one another.

I heard immense footsteps coming from the basement. It was G.I. Joe in real life if you let him tell it. G.I. Joe body slammed some cocaine on the table, looked at me, you, and my girl, and screamed, "We're going to find the rest!" almost tearing my eardrums.

43

Raw Wounds

Then he yelled, "Are there any guns in here?"

My heart skipped a few beats because I didn't know where this was heading.

"No," I said. One of those quick rebuttals that no one believes because it was voiced at turbo speed.

You said nothing.

If you ignore a pig, they go bonkers.

"Did you fuckin hear me?" he squealed, veins popping out of his face and neck.

"No yo, it aint no fuckin guns in here, damn yo," you said.

G.I. Jane marched back down the steps to go find a gun, or to plant one. I heard more thunderous banging that did nothing but thicken my anger.

My thoughts scrambled like some eggs. I felt uneasy. I went from California dreaming, feeling sunny side up to being fried up in a Baltimore nightmare. I might be young, but I've got memories to prove that I was on a first class flight to free-doom.

I have a friend named Mook who is serving a 15 year prison sentence for a house raid that he had no connection to. It was late at night and he decided to spend the night at his friend's crib. The next morning, police burst through the front door, guns out, arresting everyone in the house. Any day in the hood can be your "wrong place at the wrong time" moment in life. I felt like this was my moment.

I didn't know what you had stashed in this house. I was just embracing what was to come.

I thought back to a previous incident.

Bright lights were cutting my eyes while on stage in NYC performing my poem, "The Coldest Winter in America," when my phone started to vibrate in my pocket. I quickly hit the volume button to muffle the vibration. I finished performing my piece, sold some books, signed some autographs, gave out hugs, and took some pictures. I checked my phone: eight missed calls from Grandma. I called her back and she answered with a lump in her chest.

"Hello?"

"What's up, Grandma!?"

"The police came here looking for your brother."

I lowered my phone from my ear to my waist, gripping it, damn near cracking the screen.

"What happened? What did they find?"

I heard tears and heavy breathing on the other end.

I hung up.

I didn't have time for the bullshit, I said to myself. I went online and booked the next Greyhound bus to Baltimore. I was extremely tired, so I slept the entire ride. I got off the bus, flagged a hack, and got dropped off at the end of my block. I walked inside the house, walked up the steps and Grandma crashed into me at the top of the flight.

My first words were, "What did they find?"

She handed me a piece of paper that the officers gave her that listed all the items that were seized from the crib: a sawed off shotgun, shotgun shells, and a countless amount of stolen Apple products. You could've opened up your own store with the massive amount of Apple merchandise you had. At this point in time, you had ran away so you were staying God knows where with God knows who. I couldn't get in contact with you if I tried. I'd walk up the block and interrupt your friends' crap games and asked had they seen you. They would simply reply "Earlier" or "Nah." They were trying to preserve the ass whipping I had stashed for you.

Now, sitting in our living room, I was puzzled.

I didn't know how many pistols or birds you had nesting in here.

They lie. You lie. Who to believe? It was still the crack of dawn and I was extremely tired.

Buzz Lightyear stomped back up the steps. Now his laser was set from stun to kill. He had a 9 and a half size Jordan shoe box in his hand. The way he was carrying it, I knew it had something in it other than shoes. The box rattled like chains on a slave ship as he slammed it down on the living room table. He dug his old pale ramshackle hand in the box and pulled out three of many bullets.

Veins smothered his forehead, and the pig screamed, "Since you all lied, as soon as we find that gun, everyone in this bitch is going to jail, even Granny! I know it's a fuckin gun in here and we're gonna find it."

Bedeviled Before Birth

We know that Europeans murdered millions of Native Americans and stole their land. We know that Europeans invaded Africa and enslaved millions of Africans in this stolen land, then used racist polices and ideas, religion, "God's word" and "God's design," to justify the enslavement and murder of Africans for hundreds of years. As far back as the 1400s, Africans have been labeled by racists as "beasts" who live without a God or people who live without laws, which were the essential narratives that justified the enslavement, murder, and oppression of our ancestors. They might not call us "beasts" and "ungodly" out loud; however, racists still believe the same ideas about Black people. They think we are less human, and it justifies the racist policies that allow us to be imprisoned by the millions and murdered by the bundle. Racists believe that we as people deserve to be in caskets, jail cells, or slum-crumbled areas because there is something wrong with Black people.

MLK said, "A just law is a man-made code that squares with the moral law, or the law of God. An unjust law is a code that is out of harmony with the moral law." Many laws that are enforced by this system play a key role in the execution of Black people in America. If I shoot and kill someone, I will get charged with murder and do a prison sentence that probably would jail me for the rest of my life. However, the white police officer Betty Shelby murdered Terence Crutcher, a Black man, in Tulsa, Oklahoma, while he had his hands up. She was charged with first degree manslaughter. Betty did twenty minutes in jail and was released on a $50,000 bail.

In April of 2015, an unarmed Black man by the name of Walter Scott was recorded on video running away from the killer cop Micael Slager, who later gunned Walter down. With video evidence, the jurors on this trail said they could not "with good conscience approve a guilty verdict." As long as there is slavery and oppression, there will be racist policies and ideas to justify its wickedness. Some people will use law as a defense mechanism on Betty's or Michel's behalf and say, "What they did was legal. It was a 'justified killing.'"

When we talk about legal and illegal, remember, the enslavement and murder of Africans in America was legal at a point in history. Hanging us by trees, cutting open pregnant bellies of Black women, stomping fetuses, violently raping our men and women, locking us in chains, was "legal." Now it is no longer "legal," but loopholes still make the enslavement, murder, and oppression of Black people permissible. One of the most impactful loopholes to sustain Black enslavement, murder, and oppression in America is the 13th Amendment, which reads "The United States Constitution abolished slavery and involuntary servitude, except as punishment for a crime." This then created justification for a new slavery, by labeling Black people as criminals, and creating racist policies and ideas so that we best suit prison gear. Once again creating false perceptions that there is something wrong with Black people, and not the system.

On August 1, 2016, I was scrolling through Instagram, repeatedly seeing posts of a beautiful woman alongside hashtags that read #KorrynGaines #CityForever. I searched the hashtags and discovered that Korryn Gaines, a Baltimore City native and a fellow Baltimore City High School Alum, was gunned down by Baltimore County Police in her home. The 23-year-old woman was sitting in her home with her 5-year-old son while the police began to invade for an arrest warrant related to a traffic stop. A standoff ensued, which resulted in the officers murdering Korryn and shooting her son. Again, America for the kill.

A few days later, just after leaving a performance at a local open mic in Baltimore, I went home and took a nap. I woke up and noticed a few missed calls from a foreign number. Whoever it was left a voice mail. Initially I didn't want to check it because of the strange phone activity, messages, and voice mails I'd been receiving lately. Despite that, I still gave it a listen.

"Good morning Kondwani, this is Aleisha calling at 10:00 am on August 4th. We are getting some things together for Korryn Gaines' candle light vigil at 7:00 pm tomorrow at City High School. We wanted you to attend as a guest speaker or maybe do a poem or something. If that's something you are up for then give me a call back. Again this is Aleisha. Bye."

I reached back out to Aleisha and immediately accepted her offer.

People book me for speaking engagements and poetry performances and because of my moral obligation to social justice; I almost never turn down an opportunity unless I already have a prior engagement. January 20, 2016, I've shared the stage with Angela Davis at Radford University where we both spoke and read poetry relating to the movement and the progression of Blacks in America. December 7, 2015, I was a speaker at an alumni reception hosted by the New York City Leadership Academy at the Scholastic Headquarters. In front of 150-200 retired and current NYC principals and teachers, I provided tools on how to narrow the opportunity gap for Black and Latino students in the public school system. On August 23, 2016, I read my poetry and conducted a speech at American University's Student Welcome Week. I opened my speech with, "Regardless of your lifestyle, your ethnicity, or social class, the one thing that we all share as people, is struggle." The crowd roared and at that moment, I was connected with over one thousand students from various backgrounds. My speech then explored identity and civil rights, writing for social changes, community engagement, and refugee issues.

Any which way the pendulum of hardship swings, my writing and speaking ability will forever partake in seeking social justice for all people.

Last year when my debut poetry video #TheBaltimoreBulletTrain gained national attention, I became a highly requested speaker. The poem #TheBaltimoreBulletTrain talks about inter-communal violence. So every week, for a few months, I visited the friends and families of slain brothers or sisters to share my words. In June of 2016, popular rapper "Lor Scoota" was murdered after leaving a charity basketball game in East Baltimore. A few days later, I was asked to speak at his viewing and community appreciation event. I arrived and kids were dancing on stage singing "Chooo, I think I got the bird flu," lyrics from Scoota's song "Bird Flu," which gained the rapper national attention and success. I saw people from the ages of four to 64 either crying or doing "The Bird Flu Dance." Watching people walk in and out from viewing his body made me think about trading places with him and wondering how much easier life would be. DJs spinning all of Lor Scoota's greatest hits, jubilated kids, nosy reporters, and guys and girls laced in gold and designer clothes probably looking for a spouse.

I said my two poems and hopped off stage. I hugged a few kids who were inspired by my performance, dapped up a few old and new supporters, and did a few interviews with journalists about being a Black writer, social injustices, and community related issues. If I get a call for a brother involved in inter-communal violence, a sister involved in police violence, or any other call that inquires my help, I'll be there.

As I pulled up to my alma mater for Korryn's vigil, I saw people walking up the hill towards the school. I put my van in park, took a deep breath, said a prayer, then swallowed a few shots of mango Amsterdam. Liquor always calms my nerves down—well, at least I think it does. Since childhood, I heard my father and Grandma and other people in the hood say "I need a drink" right after something drastic happened or before something drastic was about to happen. So I guess it makes sense.

I walked through the parking lot, staring at the sky, having random thoughts about what Heaven is like, if there is one. I walked up the steps to get to where the ceremony is being held. I gave fives and hugs to people I haven't seen in years. Old classmates I use to cut class and smoke weed with. Classmates I'd sold weed to. A couple of guys I'd shot dice with in the locker room. I walked passed girls and guys whose GPAs were ranked at the top of the class; I thought they'd be doctors or lawyers but they fry chicken, work at strip clubs, or pretty much do any other job that doesn't correlate with their previous outstanding grades. I saw girls that used to do my classwork, homework, and take my exams for me. Ex-girlfriends who used to mean the world to me; now we don't speak. Ex-fuck buddies who are now pregnant, with a baby father in jail, or one that's goes up side their head every once in a while when he's doped up. People were constantly telling me how proud they are of me and how happy they are that I'm not the same person I once was in high school. They had no idea how much I felt the same way about my transformation.

I saw tears and frowns like I was at a poetry show. Instead of revolution, I smelt sorrow hanging from the trees.

I paced back and forth. People looked at me as if I had schizophrenia. I talked to myself as I got ready for my speech and poetry reading. Before I speak in front of a crowd, I get nervous. And that's exactly what was happening. I went back to my van to ease my mind. I sat in my van watching the sunset, admiring God's beauty. I pulled out my phone and started writing a poem:

A wise man once told me
"You'll have to leave her
one
day."
I couldn't fathom
We were madly in love
Our thoughts took a higher plane
God was the suppliers name
The Devil bares heat
but, God ignited these flames
Baby please don't leave
Stay for another life time, please?

The man told me that someday she has to leave
A magician couldn't see what thoughts
I thought I had under my sleeve
I begged God to let her stay and
he said "no way, all beauty must
die someday
If it wasn't for death, how
would we celebrate life?
Remember, your beautiful thing
has to die one night…"

My phone rang. It was Aleisha. "Yo Kon where you at, it's your time to speak."

I swallowed the last of the liq, went to speak, then hung in the crowd. I listened to Korryn's family and friends speak about how good of a friend and mother she was. Her father said that during the hours-long stand-off, he and other family members asked to go in and get her out because he was very certain she would listen to them. The police had said, "It's far beyond that now." The term "far beyond that now" was confirmation to me that those bullets had "Korryn Gaines" engraved on them before the standoff even begun. The racist killer cops believed that Korryn Gaines' ideal place should be six feet underground, so in their minds, she was dead long before they arrived to her home.

There were several videos of Korryn on the internet speaking out about injustices in the country dealing with Black people. She was promoting social awareness, so therefore she was a threat, and that was another justified reason for her death.

History shows that it is common for American institutions to enslave, murder, and oppress Black people, without repercussions. Too many conversations when dealing with police killing Black people involve the statement "Well what did he or she do?" Because we are conditioned to believe that there is something wrong with Black people, these murders become normal and become the fault of the victim and not the killer.

I believe any police officer who unjustly murders an individual should do time in jail. If they don't do time in jail but instead get desk duty, they should have to work for free until they retire, and the money they would have received should go to the family of the victim. Money can't replace a lost life; however, I believe that it would be a lesson learned for the killer cop and for the others to follow. We live in America where money and the lack thereof matters.

Not only do I think the killer cops should work for free, but I believe that they deserve the same punishment that they inflicted on the victim. Example: If a killer cop shoots a guy twice in the chest, that cop should receive the same. The cops that beat Freddie Gray, snapped his spinal cord, broke his voice box, and took him on a "rough ride" should be given that same punishment. If the cops live, more power to them, if he or she doesn't, oh well. I guarantee that if we implemented these consequences the amount of Blacks that are killed by police would drop because the killer cops would actually have something to lose since, now, they often keep their jobs and freedom.

Black people make up 13% of America's population, but comprise 40% of our prisons. Black males by themselves make up approximately 1,000,000 inmates in the States, which is more than India, Argentina, Canada, Lebanon, Japan, Germany, Israel, and England combined, which is roughly 740,000. If Black people make up 13% of the U.S. population, then that means we should account for somewhere close to 13% of the inmates in the U.S. prisons. Racial disparities?

During the late 1800s, separate but "equal" laws segregated nearly every aspect of life between Black and white people; ensuring Black inferiority. Because people believed that Blacks were (and still are) "uncivilized," social "problems" and "wretched," we therefore deserved to be in the worst neighborhoods in the country. We deserved to get educated in the worst schools. Along with those tragic neighborhoods and education systems, why not give us drugs to further beat us down?

After drugs were introduced to our communities, Richard Nixon started the war on drugs, only for Ronald Reagan to follow him and crack down on this war that gave out mandatory prison sentences for possession of drugs. Even though white people were using and dealing more drugs than Black people, we were still getting harsher jail sentences. If a person got caught with lower level cocaine (which was mainly used and sold in the Black communities), they received a harsher jail sentence than if caught with powder cocaine (which was mainly used and sold by whites) However, they are the same drug. This is why America can have the largest prison population in the world, and it is mostly filled with Black bodies because Black people are "criminals" and prison is where "criminals" belong. Whether or not you partake in "criminal" activities, America will find a way to throw you behind bars if you are Black. And will try to keep you out of jail if you are white.

A white rapist by the name of Brock Turner was found guilty of three felony accounts after raping a woman at Stanford University. In March 2016, a jury found him guilty of: assault with intent to commit rape of an intoxicated or unconscious person, penetration of an intoxicated person and penetration of an unconscious person.

The victim self-disclosed and said Brock raped her. There were also two random individuals who saw him behind a dumpster, half naked, taking advantage of this unconscious woman. The judge cut him some "slack" due to his lack of criminal history and his show of remorse. The judge forgot to mention his biggest escape, which was his white skin. Brock Turner's white privilege exempted him from real jail time. After a prosecutor argued he should spend six years in prison, the judge ruled he should be jailed for six months. His white privilege struck again, and he only did three months and was released in September of 2016. The judge said, "A prison sentence would have a severe impact on him." I truly wish some judges would've spared my friends and family, but because of our Blackness, it's a no go.

If Black people got the luxury of judges "sparing time" because jail has "severe impacts" on all human beings, and not just white people, other kids and I wouldn't wake up with brick-heavy tear ducts, missing our parents and friends who vanished from our neighborhoods into prison cells.

If you are Black in America, every day your freedom is up for grabs.

In 1990, a Black guy by the name of Jonathan Fleming was convicted and arrested for the murder of his friend, Daryl Rush, in New York. Fleming argued that he was on a vacation at Disney World during the time his friend Rush was murdered in 1989. Despite Fleming's evidence of videos, post cards, and a plane ticket to Florida, the prosecution argued that he could have flown back to NY, killed Rush, and returned to Disney World. A witness testified to seeing Fleming committing the murder. Later on, the witness admitted to falsely accusing him to get her own charges dropped. The prosecutors said she was lying, so they ignored her claim. In 2013, the case reopened and in 2014, after spending over two decades in prison, Fleming was released and exonerated: new evidence showed that he was in Florida hours before the murder took place. Fleming's Black skin robbed him of over twenty years of his life. Good job, America.

In 2010, Kalief Browder, a Black sixteen-year-old, was arrested and charged with a robbery that he did not commit. This resulted in him spending three years on Rikers Island, waiting for a trial that never happened. Browder spent two of those years in solitary confinement, where he was cramped in windowless rooms for 24 hour days, which inflicted him with psychological pain. When he did have contact with humans, it was brutal. He was beaten by inmates and correctional officers regularly. He attempted suicide on several occasions while incarcerated. A few months after he was released in 2013, innocent, he attempted suicide again. Browder was in and out of psychiatric hospitals, which was smothering his attempts of suicide, until he later got the job done in June 2015. It's no doubt that his traumatic experiences at Rikers Island was the cause of his mental instability, which resulted in him taking his own life. Another murder of a Black person with America's blood all over it.

If there are two doorways diverged in your direction and you choose the "right" one, your days can still be cut short like Kalief, Jonathan, or the millions of other Black people that America's racist system has enslaved, murdered, and oppressed. America is a place where you can do "all of the right things," succeeding to unimaginable heights. But when racism strikes, your Black skin can chop away chunks of your life.

* * *

Growing up in East Baltimore, I realized that talking about personal mental instability is frowned upon. I remember I was 13 years old sitting on Tench Tilghman Elementary's ancient run-down playground equipment, cracking open liquor bottles, emptying blunt guts, preparing to get oven baked. I was accompanied by two friends, Lor Chris and Fat Head. Fat Head got his name because his head was a bag of bricks. I hit the blunt first, swung it over to Lor Chris, then he swung it over to Fat Head. Right after he hit the blunt, he said, "Yo, I got a lot of shit on my mind."

"Yeah I can tell, a lot of heavy shit, too," I said, clowning him about that boulder he has on his neck. Me and Lor Chris rolled on the ground, laughing.

Fat Head silenced us by yelling, "Yo, I'm not jokin, I really be feeling fucked up."

I seized my laughing and said, "How?"

"I don't know."

"How don't you know?" said Lor Chris, cutting him off.

"Yo, let him finish talking," I said.

"When I be sleep sometimes I be having nightmares of when I seen my farva get killed. I only sleep for like two hours a night. That shit keep me up. It be hard for me to eat sometimes. I be twitching and shit. Sweating and shit."

"Did you ever talk to your mother about it?" I said.

"Yeah, but she just tell me to stay strong and don't be telling nobody because they gonna think I'm crazy and shit."

If the words "stay strong" were the antidote for problems, I believe that all of us would be healed from our mental trauma.

Fat Head's mother is every other parent, friend, and family member in the hood who tells someone to "stay strong" and "get over" their mental trauma. We are told to just deal with tragedy but never taught how to aid the damage. Just like Fat Head, many of us go through life shattered, using drugs, alcohol, lust, and other janky remedies to ease our pain.

After Fat Head spilled out his heart, I started to wonder if we were suffering from the same "thing." I experienced sleepless nights, rapid heart beating, wicked flashbacks, and unwanted suicidal thoughts. Could Fat Head and I be drowning in the same murky water?

I, too, was about to spill out my heart and tell him that he wasn't alone. As soon as I found the words to say, I tossed them out my memory bank, swallowed some liquor and said, "You'll be okay nigga, just pass the blunt."

During wartime, soldiers exchange blows and bullets, then later get diagnosed with Post Traumatic Stress Disorder. PTSD is a mental health disorder that develops after experiencing or witnessing life-threatening events. Our entire lives, my childhood friends and I have been seeing blood, broken bones, brains, and guts splattered on sidewalks. In our neighborhoods, people swing pistols, baseball bats, knives, and bare knuckles, religiously. We were not the only group of young poor Black boys and girls experiencing this in America. Did society think that we would not be mentally affected? We've been enduring trauma since we had milk on our breath. Flashbacks, nightmares, and monstrous memories still trouble me. And seeing our brothers and sisters shot dead, beaten, and raped across the country on the internet isn't healing this trauma any faster, especially living in Baltimore, where there is an annual homicide rate of roughly 300 people.

Trauma is constantly strong-armed onto the spines of poor people in America. If "All Lives Matter," then they would receive the same mental aid as the American soldiers who have survived combat. If you don't believe that all groups of people deserve the same support, then you perpetuate class racism.

Since I'm here, I'll talk about the issue of people saying things such as "All Lives Matter" or "Black Lives won't matter until they matter to Black people." Let me first address the fact that "All Lives Matter" was a counter-statement to "Black Lives Matter" becoming a slogan and movement. So where was "All Lives Matter" our entire stay here in America?

When there is a fire, and firefighters rush in the home, spraying water to silence the flames, there is never a group of people rushing out of an alley saying, "Hey, what are you guys doing? Don't you know that all houses matter?" This is what people saying "All Lives Matter" in response to "Black Lives Matter" sound like.

Only an idiot and a person who doesn't know their history will say, "Black people don't care about Black life." That statement is another false idea that promotes Black people's inferiority—a group of people who are incapable of feeling grief. Is it because the media chooses to share with the world Black people uprising for police-involved murders? The world doesn't see or hear the stories across the country of people putting in blood, sweat, and tears to help prevent inter-communal killings. The world doesn't know about people creating resources to improve impoverished neighborhoods that were constructed by America's racist policies and ideas.

Just because someone's anger or compassion isn't channeled the way you think it should, doesn't mean they don't care.

I've been to several funerals where anger exploded like sodas in the freezer because it has been bottled up for ages. I have seen family, friends, and even pastors get dropped by quick jabs. While their sons are being lowered into the ground, I have seen drunken fathers jump in the grave, wailing, "I want to be buried with my son." I even know of some people who committed suicide after losing a loved one to violence.

But Black Lives don't matter to Black people? Only misinformed people would say that; in my community, and in other communities around the country, Black life has always, and will continue to, have substantial value.

Not everyone has the same practices when it comes to dealing with death and mourning the dead. Some Indonesians keep the corpses of their family members in their homes, still involving them in daily routines: dinner, discussions, and prayer. Some cultures in America prefer open casket funerals, some prefer cremations. Some cultures have celebratory dinners or parties. My culture gets "Rest in Peace" t-shirts and dog tags with pictures of our slain loved one on them. We go to the funeral, leave, then pour liquor on the curb for our fallen homies above, and indulge in other drugs. Just because you don't witness or understand a person's grieving methods does not invalidate their pain.

Little brother, I know you've seen 34 years of pain during your 17 years of life. We have to first address and advocate for our own mental health issues so we can receive the proper treatment for the betterment of our people. Because if we wait on someone else, we'll be waiting forever. One day I'm going to seek some professional help because I believe that it can improve mental instabilities. But for now, I'll continue to flood my liver with light liquor. It got me this far.

* * *

It was December 30, 2003. My little brother Fidel, his older brother Davon, other childhood friends, and myself played on our block with our new Christmas toys. Cheap remote controlled cars that lasted a few weeks, footballs that got lost in a day or so, bicycles that came with instructions from parents—"Don't let nobody hold your fuckin bike"—and several other gifts and gadgets. Nighttime approached. We had to go in the house.

I asked, "Grandma, can Fidel stay over tonight?"

"No, he live across the damn street. Ya'll can see each other tomorrow."

I always wondered why my little brother Fidel and his mother lived directly across the street from us. He and Davon both stayed with their mother Tiffany; we stayed with Grandma. Fidel and I had the same father. Fidel and Davon had the same mother.

My father had two baby mothers living across the street from one another. How does that happen? I never asked questions about that until I got older. One random day, I asked Mommy how she and Tiffany ended up living on the same block.

Mommy said, "Me and Tiffany was beefin' and I remember she said to me during our beef, 'Keep crackin slick bitch. I got something for you,' and then next thing you know she moved on the block."

I thought that was one of the funniest things ever. Mommy and Tiffany never got along during my childhood. Mommy used to always say, "That bitch Tiffany is jealous of my son," referring to me. I remember I was a small child, kneeling down looking out of my window watching Tiffany get her ass whipped by Mommy. Mommy's connecting right hooks and jabs was knocking Tiffany's head all over the place. Mommy was probably 110 pounds, if that. Tiffany was probably pushing 250. I think this is the first time I realized that size didn't matter in a fistfight. I vividly remember Mommy dragging Tiffany across the concrete, by her hair, pulling out handfuls of cheap weave, serving her blows by the second. Tiffany got beat so bad that she lied to the police and said that Mommy and Auntie jumped her, when I don't think our aunt has ever been in a fight a day in her life. One thing I can say about Mommy is that she was a real G. Her tiny ass could fight and she wasn't scared of anything or anyone. I've personally seen Mommy fuck people up: ex-boyfriends, girlfriends, associates, enemies, etc. People tell me all the time how Mommy used to whip everybody's ass back in the day, even the guys. Their exact words were, "Boy, your mother got hands like a nigga." I even remember being laid up with a shorty and I got a call from a homeboy who said, "Yo, you need to come home. Your mother is around here wild'n. She hit some bitch in the head with a brick." I left the shorty's crib, pulled up to my home, and their mommy was. Sitting on the curb in handcuffs, getting ready to take that oh so familiar journey to Central Bookings. I could sit here and write you a storehouse full of stories that I experienced, however, it would take much more than a letter.

Whatever differences Tiffany and Mommy had never affected the relationship between me and my little brother Fidel. Although Grandma wasn't gonna let Fidel stay the night, it was still the best feeling in the world to live across the street from one of my best friends.

"Please Grandma! Pretty please." I begged and begged for her to let Fidel stay at our house.

She still said no. "That damn boy ain't staying over here when his ass live across the street."

My sad puppy face usually gets Grandma going, but this time it didn't work. The night was coming to a close and Fidel, Davon, and I finished playing around. We dapped each other up, shared hugs, and went inside our separate homes.

That next morning, at approximately 4:00 am, I heard King Kong knocking on the door. I woke suddenly, and thought to myself, "It's probably a junkie." The knocking stopped. I went back to sleep. A few minutes later, the knocks returned like an outbreak. Grandma shot downstairs to the front door. I got out of my bed, eye gunk still gluing my lids shut, and blindly followed her. I looked out the front door with my head resting on Grandma's waist.

Across the street were heavy dark clouds of smoke oozing out of a home. It was my little brother's Fidel bedroom window. The knocks I heard were coming from Fidel's mother Tiffany. Running up and down the block in a long white t-shirt, shoeless, thumping on every door on the block, screaming, trying to wake someone to call an ambulance for her two sons, who were drowning in flames. Ambulances and fire trucks stormed the block, moving as fast as they could. Fire fighters extended their ladders, burst open windows and ripped roofs off like wigs. They pulled a flimsy salmon pink object out of the flames, which ended up being Fidel. Some minutes later, they pulled out Davon.

"They found one of the boys under his bed," the officials said, "and the other in a corner."

"The hearts of both boys had stopped beating," said *The Baltimore Sun*, who covered an article about the house fire.

The next day, I had walked to Johns Hopkins Hospital to visit Fidel. At this point, Davon had already succumbed to his injuries and died in the hospital before I had chance to see him. This was by far, my worst New Year's experience ever. This is why it is nearly impossible for me to get into the Christmas and New Year's spirit; ever since this tragedy, there hasn't been a year that hasn't haunted me.

I sat in the waiting room with friends and family, watching everyone trying to hold themselves together. I didn't shed any tears but I was crying monsoons on the inside. I heard a loud beep and it drew my eyes toward the elevator.

It was my father in handcuffs accompanied by two police officers. My father was in prison serving a sentence. Sometimes prisoners get passes when a family member has died or is undergoing life-threatening surgeries.

Seeing my pops made my visit a little better. It'd been a while since I'd seen him. He stood there with his black boots, and his light blue pants and shirt that read "D.O.C" on the back. He smiled at me and I returned, even a bigger smile. I ran towards him and gave him a mile-long hug. The officers looked at me strangely; not understanding the love a young boy has for his father who he might never see again.

As happy as I was, I knew that seeing him was a tease. We sat down for a bit and caught up on "life," not that I knew much about it. We talked until the doctor called us back to see Fidel.

The walk to his room was a long one. We arrived and there he was, unconscious. All of the hair on his head, gone. His face was swollen like a pregnant belly. Blisters the size of boiled eggs covered his face. Tubes voyaged through his throat, nose, penis, and other body parts. I slowly stuck out my hand, shaking like a bum with a cup full of change, and touched him. A few tears belly flopped onto his face. I felt a hand touch my shoulder and heard a voice say, "Talk to him, he can hear you."

It was my father. I thought it was strange talking to a dead body, well an almost dead body.

"He can't hear me; he's dead."

"He's not dead. He's just in a deep sleep," my father said.

I started to helplessly whisper his name as I began to shake him slightly. "Fidel...Fidel."

Something just didn't feel right. I shook him a little harder, my voice got a little louder.

"Fidel!...Fidel!"

He still didn't wake up. I've never met anyone in my life in a sleep as deep as this one.

My father and the doctor were speaking about Fidel's condition. I didn't understand the big adult words they were using, so I left and headed back to the waiting room. I shed a few more tears and started to ask myself, "I wonder when I'm going to die?"

This was my first time experiencing a tragic death with a close family member. Not only experiencing this grief, but literally seeing the fire occur and then watching his scorching pink body being pulled out of the flames. It scarred me. I still have nightmares. The smell of burnt flesh still lingers in my nostrils and his salmon pink body still tap dances on my eyeballs.

I spent a little more time with my father until it was his time to go. As he was departing, I started to feel lonely. Wondering when I will see him again. Maybe never. Many young Black boys and girls in the hood have fathers that leave without notice. Sometimes they come back, most of the time they never do.

I miss you, Dad. I hope to see you soon.

Later the next day, I received a call from my Grandmother and she spoke in a tone that still haunts me to this day.

She said, "Fidel died…We had to pull the plug."

I didn't say anything for the next minute or so. I then hung up the phone, ran upstairs, and spent my tears on inconsiderate pillows that gave me nothing back in return. "Why my little brother?" I asked. A question I battle with daily. He was only seven years old. What could he have possibly done wrong for his karma to be as such? When tragic incidents happen to the innocent, it makes me question if karma is a real thing or not.

Fidel and Davon's mother Tiffany failed to pay her gas and electric bill, so she let her kids use candles for light. The fire started when the candles fell to the bathroom floor, igniting the entire upstairs where Fidel and Davon slept. Meanwhile, their mother awoke in the basement, peeped the fire, and fled. Because the house had no power, they did not have a working phone, which is why she ran out, screaming and thumping on doors for help.

Sometimes I get upset when I think about Fidel. Quite often, I wish that Fidel was here. When I think about the bullshit he doesn't have to deal with in this world, I began to feel a little better.
At least he was the first one to make it out the hood. The first one to make it out of this man-made Hell.

You know I am the oldest of seven, so I was blessed with having the responsibility to set the foundation for my younger siblings. That's a tough job for anyone, especially a young Black man in America. Sometimes I wonder was Fidel's death my fault. Maybe I should've begged Grandma a little harder and she would've finally said yes. Or I should've stayed the night with him at his place and we could've died together. Ever since that fire, everyone keeps saying, "God wanted this to happen. Fidel and Davon's deaths were in his plans."

That is a statement that I never understood and I probably won't ever understand. People even use that statement to justify the enslavement, murder, and oppression of Black people in America. It's hard for me to believe that the omnibenevolent God incorporated the enslavement, ill-treatment, and massacre of Black people in his "master plan." That's such a horrible thing to do.

There are plenty of parents in this world who don't have their priorities together. Your unorganized priorities can result in your children being slighted on opportunities, resources, clothes, food, and in some cases like Fidel and Davon, they can end up dead. Growing up in Baltimore, I've seen parents go to the club faithfully but never make one parent teacher night. I've seen parents pay every drug dealer in the hood attention but couldn't pay their bills. Living beyond your means can kill your kids. I've seen it happen. All of my parents out there who are slacking when it comes to putting your child's wellbeing first, tighten up. Or you might be the reason for your child's demise.

* * *

It was a Friday. Blood was dripping like Jheri curl juice and tears leaked like broken fire hydrants. Keisha's boyfriend James struck again. This wasn't the first time James hit Keisha with a few uppercuts and massive right hooks like Muhammad Ali. For many moons, he'd been splitting Keisha's shit wide open like crackhouses on the first of the month. There had been several occasions where I'd seen Keisha carrying black eyes, bruised lips, and other scarred body parts.

I was thinking about how I should get my cousin Rod to knock James' teeth down his throat with the back of a sawed-off. Or about how I should take it upon myself, kidnap him, tie him up in a warehouse, force feed him spoiled milk and rotten bananas and let him shit on himself until his insides roll out the crack of his ass. Or have a few of my little homies sneak in his home and bleach all of his fake Gucci and Hermes clothing. Or take a hammer to a screwdriver, and knock out all of his teeth one by one. Or beat him in the face with a brick until he was unidentifiable to his own mother. But I digress, because violence isn't the answer for all problems. However, there is nothing I hate more than a man putting his hands on an innocent woman.

Malcolm X said, "A people who are blind to the truth about their enemies, will seek to embrace or integrate with that enemy."

As I write this, Keisha is still in a relationship with James. (If he hasn't killed her already.)

Carter G. Woodson said, "If you can control a man's thinking you do not have to worry about his actions. If you make a man think that he is justly an outcast, you do not have to order him to the back door. He will go without being told; and if there is no back door, his very nature will demand one." I hear this and think about people who are being controlled, people who are trapped by their circumstances because an outside force restrains their mind.

In life, we all are manipulated by the art of misdirection. It's not about being misdirected, it's about how long you are misdirected. A caged mind can become free. A free mind can become whatever it chooses.

I don't believe there is a law or scripture anywhere on this planet that can fully support and make sense of oppressors living happy and unified lives amongst the oppressed. Do you think that bloodthirsty wolves can live amongst sheep and dwell together in unity without the wolves having the sheep for lunch? No. So why would anyone believe that any group of oppressed people will get the freedom they deserve while living in a place where polices and ideas continue to enslave, murder, and oppress them?

I've heard many people say, "An entire group of people departing a country to relocate is far-fetched. It's impossible. We have everything here in America already; who's gonna wanna leave? Black on Black violence will happen no matter where they relocate."

But I ask this: What good is longevity if the entire journey was horrific? The term "Black on Black violence" drills a hole in my temple. "Black on Black violence" is a stigmatic term that is used to demote the humanization of Black people who are involved in "criminal" activity. The term is actually "inter-communal violence," which is violence existing or occurring between people of the same community. White people who live amongst other whites, kill white people, just as Asians kill other Asians, and so on. You never hear the term "white on white crime" when in actuality, white people kill more whites than Blacks who kill Blacks.

This society pushes the perception that people of color are more violent than others. We have been conditioned to use and accept the term "Black on Black violence" as if it is a real thing. We need to admit that this term is used to animalize and demote the humanization of Black people and then we need to strip it off of our tongues.

Leaving America won't abolish violence because, like God, violence is omnipresent. There isn't sunshine in Heaven every day. Remember, Lucifer once lived there.

* * *

The racist policies and ideas that justified the enslavement, murder, and oppression of Africans in America created the perfect opportunity for the justification of Korryn Gaines, Terrence Crutcher, Walter Scott, Freddie Gray and every other Black person who has been murdered by the police, and the ones who will get murdered in the future. These racist policies and ideas also created the perfect opportunity for Jonathan Fleming and Kalief Browder to serve years in prison for crimes they did not do, while Brock Turner, a white rapist, can do virtually no time in prison for raping a woman. These examples are a single strand of hair on the head of racism in America.

In 1829, David Walker, an African American abolitionist and "anti-slavery activist," said, "Blacks were the most degraded, wretched, and abject beings who ever lived since the world began." This explains the false barbaric imagery that continues to eat away at Black life here in America. You can be a racist white person, or a pro-black "activist," and produce and consume racist policies and ideas. As long as this happens, your Black skin will not ever matter in America. So don't be surprised the next time a Black person is wrongfully murdered, thrown in prison, or mistreated in any form or fashion, and there are no repercussions for the victimizer.

America. Home of the slaves.

I begin to shake my head as I watched Officer Dick Head turn watermelon red. Side note: I never understood why white people called Black people colored when white people turn red, blue, and pink, depending on their mood. But I digress.

My tongue became heavy like burdens. I tried to talk but I couldn't. Then lions ran out of my mouth at breakneck speed.

"What the fuck is wrong with you yo!?"

You sat there with a mile-long attitude as if all of this wasn't your fault. Maybe it wasn't. Maybe it was mine. Maybe if I would worked a little harder, I could've made enough money to get us out of the hood. Maybe I should've been a more involved big brother.

I should've intervened more when I saw you digging your own grave with the same shovel that your father and mother used.

The bacon smugglers went back downstairs and left us with this stubby Asian lieutenant who was filling out paperwork.

Besides the demise of this family, I kept thinking about the two shows I had this weekend in Virginia and New York. One thing I loathe is canceling and backing out of shows, especially if the reason of not showing up involved going to jail.

I started to think about the news headlines and what they would say after I got arrested. "Poet Laureate turned crack dealer." "Guns and Gospel." "Rapper Kondwani Fidel uses poetry to mask drug trafficking." "22 year old poet using his 75 year old grandmother's house to store crack." "What would Malcolm X think of this crack dealing activist?" "Famous substitute teacher is slinging hope and dope." "Did he have dreams of becoming Langston Hughes or Pablo Escoabar?"

If I wanted to deal with this bullshit, I would've never went to college and just kept selling drugs in East Baltimore. Watching junkies fight each other over the last free pill I decided to give away before I closed shop. Running around making sure I don't get caught by Grandma. Making sure my father or any of his friends didn't see me. Sitting on the block eating frozen cups. Eating chicken boxes smothered in salt, pepper, and ketchup and a jumbo half and half. Girl-

friends sliding in and out the block in their new whips. This was my reality. The block first started calling me when my greatest challenge was tracing my name for homework assignments. It was set up for me to stay complacent and fail, but I made it through. I just don't want the same life for you. You might not be as lucky as I was, and make it out.

I started to think about those guys who tell those stories about who they could've been. I'd be that guy doing years in prison saying, "I used to be…I got a degree in…I'm really not supposed to be in here…What had happened, was…" An entire load of bullshit that no one cares about. I hated those kind of dudes. Therefore, I wasn't looking forward to being one of them. But who knows, life tends to go all the way left when you're doing all of the right things.

The officer that looked like Arnold Schwarzenegger from Terminator, with black glasses and spiked brown hair, said, "You're a stupid nigger, living in a crackhouse and you have a college degree?"

I said nothing.

Your big ass lips just couldn't stay fastened.

"What you talking about? This ain't no crack house!"

The pigs went berserk, shouting over top of one another. "The fuck you mean, it's crack in here, isn't it, dumb ass?"

Grandma always preached to us, "We can all sing at the same time. We can't all talk at the same time."

So as they were yelling, I could only imagine how disgusted Grandma was on the inside.

Just as much as I want to whip your little black scrawny ass, I want to love you. Give you that love that our mother never strangled us with. That love that your father fumbled.

Granny sat there helpless. You could see it in her eyes that she's seen situations like this too many times and saying that she's upset is an understatement. Every time something hits the fan, I always think about how Grandma probably dreamed to go on vacations and enjoy a happy life with a husband and all of the other things that women like, yet she's involved in another house raid. She adopted us out of the kindness of her heart and this is how we repay her?

She had that look of sorrow that's silently howling, and the only words she could seem to scrape up during this entire situation were, "I'm tired."

Those years of praying she did for all of her babies have officially fell short.

The Asian cop asked you, "Is that your room downstairs?"

You replied. "Yes."

"So the bullets and coke is all yours?"

"Yes."

Time stopped. I stopped. I went into a deep thought.

They went downstairs and grabbed an outfit for you to put on. They helped dress you, then guided you out. PNB Rock's song "Too Many Years" played in my head:

"I swear I done shed too many tears, for niggas that I won't get back.
I got niggas in the graveyard, niggas in the state yard, I swear not a day goes by.
That I don't think about the times, I wish that I could rewind."

There are so many instances in my life that I wish I could rewind. Rewind and try my best to stop my friends and family from being murdered and thrown in jail.

Granny wanted you to go to jail because she thought it'd be the best place for you. We live in a world where grandparents think it'll be better off for their kids and grandkids to be in jail than in the streets, not knowing that both environments are forms of slavery. One just has a few more bars. The look of grief on Grand-mas's face was triggering a bizarre emotion. I didn't know if I wanted to cry or laugh at this all. I sat, still handcuffed, and watched you depart.

You were gently following down the path that society has set out for you. Your footprints in the sand were some heavy ones. I know that one day you will become free. I just pray that you do, before it's too late.

Backbone of Athanasia

I was on my way to NYC for the book release celebration for the paperback version of the New York Times Bestseller *The Beast Side*. I love attending celebratory events. If I'm being honest, I only love attending events that have free food and liquor. This one was right up my alley. As soon as I walked in, a short white guy with brown hair asked to take my coat. I gave it to him, then allowed my nose to guide me to the food. The first thing that caught my eye was a sign that said "Fells Point Crab Cakes." I burst into laughter because I knew damn well that they didn't have Fells Point Crab Cakes in New York. You and I both know that Fells Point is a waterfront neighborhood in Baltimore with several small restaurants and pubs, and is famous for its seafood and signature crab cakes. I kind of took it as whoever made these crab cakes and the phony crab cake sign was doing it as a welcoming gesture for the Baltimore-based author, whose work we were celebrating. My appetite didn't let me turn the phony crab cakes down, so I devoured about five of them, along with nachos, dip, and washed it all down with several cups of white wine. I did some networking, shared a few laughs with some new and old friends, and ate more finger food.

After the event, I hopped on the next bus back home to Baltimore. Fifteen minutes out on the highway, I instantly became depressed. It seems that at the end of my best days, I succumb to life's pressures. I feel like I have no friends, future, and no God. I sat there in my seat and felt my emotions creeping down on me. After about thirty minutes on the highway, I started to break down crying. Although the cry was silent, tears drenched my jeans. Suicide then swarmed my brain and she began calling the shots. I cried, and cried, and cried. I rapidly unzipped my back pack, and yanked out a bottle of prescription pills. I wanted to get rid of this pain. A pain that has been slowly destroying me for years. Pain that goes away and comes back time to time whenever it wants. The pain is like Mother Nature, unpredictable.

I eye balled the pill bottle and wondered about all of the people who would miss me when I'm gone. However, that didn't stop me from what I was about to do. I pushed down the top on the bottle then twisted to the left, popping it open then popping a pill, followed by a small gulp of water. I popped a second pill, drunk a little a water. Popped a third pill, no water. A fourth pill, no water. This fourth pill got stuck sliding down my throat which made me gag up a little vomit along with the pill. I took the pill, slammed it to the back of my throat, and swallowed it for a second time with the vomit that was used as a tool to soften the swallow.

This didn't stop my pain. This didn't stop my tears. I cried. I cried some more until my tear ducts became empty and dry. I slid into a deep nod with the taste of tears on my tongue. The nod became deeper by the second. I felt my eyes roll to the back of head and it was all over.

No more pain. No more problems. No more heartache.

Until I was awakened by a loud "Get up man. This is the last stop. You gotta get off."

I wasn't upset that the bus driver woke me up; I was upset that he had the ability to wake me up—because I wasn't dead. I knew that I should've popped eight pills instead of four. What was I thinking? However, I stumbled off the bus, called an Uber, and headed home. I went into the house and began to feel the same pain that I experienced on my bus ride.

"I'm going to pop the whole fuckin bottle this time," I said to myself. I dug into my bag for the pills, just to realize that I left them on the bus.

* * *

Growing up without positive parents will show you how much parents cost. The causes of my heartache and pain isn't limited to my parents. Much of my anger stems from the inhumane circumstances that enslave, murder, and oppress Black people in this country. For a long period of time I have chosen not to speak about many of my own vulnerabilities because I thought people would label me as "weird" or a "freak." Throughout my journey in life, I started finding myself more and more every day. I started loving myself more and more every day. I started accepting myself more and more every day. This resulted in me being unafraid and unapologetically myself.

I accepted the life of a writer, which plagued me with a great volume of anger as well. James Baldwin said, "To be a Negro in this country and to be relatively conscious is to be in rage almost all the time."

One night, I was at the bar drinking, talking with my uncle about being a Black writer. We took some shots, talked about the old days, and shared some laughs. Randomly, he said, "Are you sure this is what you wanna do with your life? You know people get killed over this shit."

I knew that he and other family members and friends were scared for my well-being. I responded to my uncle with a quote from Huey P. Newton: "The first lesson a revolutionary must learn is that he is a doomed man…My fear is not death itself but death without a meaning."

He then looked at me as if I were insane. I told him that I didn't yearn to be a writer and to speak about the inequalities in America, but on the other hand, writing found me. I understood that my people needed my assistance, and I believe that I would've been a disservice to my people and to God if I didn't use my gift to fight with them in this struggle we face here in America. I'm prepared to die. I know for a fact that I'm going to die while engaged in this struggle with my people in America. If our ancestors didn't risk and lose their lives for freedom, then we would still be in chains. And don't you ever think that the oppressors plan to say, "You know what? I think they had enough. Let's ease up off of them a little."

Nobody is going to put your wants, needs, and emotions over their own self-interest. Like I wrote before, money and lack thereof matters greatly in America. There are big bucks in oppressing people. When someone gets thrown behind prison bars, someone else receives a check. When someone gets murdered by the police, someone else receives a check. When one of our brothers or sisters is slain in the streets, someone else receives a check. When we die slow from eating cancerous foods, someone else receives a check. When drug addicts overdose and die, someone else receives a check.

The enslaved suffers while the slave masters reap all of the money and benefits that get generated.

For quite some time now, death threats have been my norm, and I believe Federal Agents have presented themselves. Going into details won't be necessary. But what are they looking for? The same thing they look for when anyone tells the truth. When I first picked up a pen, I never thought that my words would make people want my head on a chopping block.

Huey P. Newtown said, "Black men and women who refuse to live under oppression are dangerous to white society because they become symbols of hope to their brothers and sisters, inspiring them to follow their example." If you don't maintain terror, then an empire is doomed. Black women and men who refuse to live under oppression are labeled as terrorists by the oppressors. So therefore it doesn't matter how big or small you are. A threat is a threat. And I'm a threat. Do I intend to be a threat? No. I just speak my truth, and if that is threatening to you, then stand threatened. I am not the first and definitely not the last person who will be targeted for speaking up against social injustices in this country.

While trying to stay mindful of my surroundings and dealing with being who I truly am, I have a boatload of other things which include: me being a "good" brother to my younger siblings. Being a "good" man to keep a woman happy. Being a "good" grandson. Being a "good" son. Being a "good" friend to all of my homies.

I am no longer that little Koni who used to play soccer and basketball. I'm not that little Koni who got perfect attendance and honor roll every quarter in elementary school. I'm not that little Koni who ran through hallways in elementary school causing havoc during quiet time. I'm not that little Koni who used to run in and out of corner stores and steal Doritos and packs of bubble gum. I'm not that little Koni who smoked weed from sunrise till sunset. I'm not that little Koni who ran around East Baltimore at twelve years old, chasing girls, trying to lose my virginity. I'm not that little Koni who cried for McFlurries from McDonalds and couldn't get it because I didn't have "McDonald's money." I'm not that little Koni who spent his first paycheck on gold teeth and tattoos. I'm not that little Koni who broke girls' hearts in high school. I'm not that little Koni who shot dice and sold snacks in the hallways and locker rooms. I'm not that little Koni who was selling heroin and crack to my people. I am now Kondwani Fidel, a young man who wants to give back to his people.

I am no longer that guy that you once knew. So only if it means anything to you, understand the person who I am today.

Jay-Z said, "Everybody look at you strange, say you changed. Like you work that hard to stay the same." I will only become more resilient and even a better writer, and to America, even a much bigger threat.

I have a hustle and spirit that is undeniable. It's not for self-gain, but for the love I have for the people. That's why young girls and guys snapchat me from Africa congratulating me on the inspiration I give them. That's why people from the UK send me Facebook and Instagram messages telling me how I might never meet them and they might not ever fully understand the Black struggle in America, but they love that I'm fighting for a cause. That's why I get messages from people who reside across the country, telling me that my poetry helped ease their mental illness.

People all over the world reach out to me constantly and tell me how much of an influence I am to the world and why they thank God for my existence. My ability to motivate and empower people speaks for itself.

No matter your religion, ethnicity, or social class, we all struggle. Someone in this world needs you. I'm not telling you not to cry, but after you let out that anger and frustration, wipe those tears and handle your business. Pick up your weapon and fight. If it's a pair of boxing gloves, a paint brush, ballet shoes, a basketball, a college degree, a microphone, or a pen—grab it and get to work. Fight your way to liberation.

Another key to fighting a good fight is to have a champion-like friend in your corner at all times. Someone you can look to for guidance when you're lost. Find a person who will keep you alive on your worst days. I've found my person, and I believe that her spirit can heal a universe of broken people.

On March 5, 2008, at the age of 13, my friend Tiarnee was diagnosed with Renal Cell Carcinoma, which is a rare kidney cancer. Tiarnee currently works at Johns Hopkins Hospital, the same hospital where she was supped to die at 13. Today, she is a physical therapist technician. Tiarnee hasn't beat cancer yet, but she will. Tiarnee frequently calls me her hero when in all actuality she is mine. Tiarnee is a warrior in every sense of the word. Our lives might not be the party we wished for, however, while we're here, the least we can do is two step. Tiarnee is two stepping.

If she can make the best out of her situation, then anyone else can do the same. You too can have that same champion-like spirit as Tiarnee. A real man or woman makes the best out of the situations they are placed in. For a number of years, since Africans landed on the shores of America, we have proved to ourselves that we can stay jubilant and iron-willed through a train wreck of troubles: enslavement, murder, and oppression. Once I asked Tiarnee if she was afraid of death, and she erupted, "Hell no! But I do look at the world differently because I was supposed to die at 13. I'm not going anywhere no time soon. I will never say 'cancer beat me.' I can't leave even if I wanted to because if I quit it's gonna affect people in a negative way and make others want to quit."

From our ancestors to Tiarnee to you. Running from the worst of your problems will not save you. See it through. Resilience is key.

* * *

On April 12, 1860, Jefferson Davis, a great racist and U.S. senator from Mississippi, gave a speech where he addressed a bill that wanted to give money for the advancement of education to Black people in DC. In his speech, he said, "This government was not founded by negroes nor for negroes, but by white men for white men." Then he stated, "The inequalities between the Black and white races was stamped from the beginning."

I blame America for its long history of racist policies and ideas that enslaved, murdered, and oppressed Black people, which made Black opportunities inferior. Every wretched environment in America, whether city schools, prisons, neighborhoods, or in front of a cop's gun— is where the producers and consumers of racists ideas and polices believe that Black people best fit. Every struggle that Black people endure in America is a symptom of the initial enslavement of African people. A selection of white men in America took it upon themselves, not to create a Heaven on earth, but a Heaven for themselves, and a man-made Hell for Black people.

Pay attention. Not once have I blamed "the white man" for anything. But in history there have been some white men who were in control of the enslavement, oppression, and murder of African people in America. These select white men produced racist policies and ideas that dehumanized Africans in America. These policies and ideas created a system that unconsciously and automatically nourishes a racist psychology and behaviorism in not only white men, but many women and men of all different backgrounds. We will never not see color in America until all people, no matter their different color skin, hair, religion, sexual preference, or gender are seen and treated like human beings.

Africans were labeled "barbaric" and "devilish" and "cursed by God," which legalized the enslavement of them. Africans were viewed as "devilish," so making them slaves and "saving" their souls, forcing Christianity upon them, was the right thing to do.

Korryn Gaines, Freddie Gray, Trayvon Martin, Walter Scott, Joe McKnight and every other Black person who was murdered and didn't receive justice was fitting for those fatalities they succumbed to: the media depicted them as "thugs" and "criminals," and that's the reason they don't deserve to be living amongst regular humans. As long as Black people are viewed as less human, America will always find strategies to keep us padlocked to poverty, prison, and graveyards.

It has always been drilled in the heads of Americans who produce and consume racist policies and ideas that it is something wrong with Black people, and not the administration that has enslaved, murdered, and oppressed Black people.

I am not scared of this system, nor am I afraid of the people who are in control, nor am I afraid of the future. A Black writer will always face scrutiny in America. You can't name one person who stood for a positive change in the world that didn't receive any hate.

Despite the Black oppression in America, my lack of being a "good" family member, my mental instabilities, death threats, and other societal dilemmas, I vow to never put anything over the interest of my people in the struggle. Not only the Black struggle, but all struggles. I will always attempt to best express the vast clarity of the dark shadows clouding the lives and opportunities of people in the struggle. I will constantly be a voice for the tongueless streets as long as God gives me breath. Even if he takes it away, I hope that my words linger longer than the smell of rottenness in this country.

While writing this book, I tried my best to tell the truth in ways for you to understand.

Toni Morrison said, "This is precisely the time when artists go to work. There is no time for despair, no place for self-pity, no need for silence, no room for fear. We speak, we write, we do language. That is how civilizations heal."

I will continue to try and heal the raw wounds that infect me and others in the world. I will continue to evolve. I will continue to fight.

I hope this song provides an immortal rhythm that you can always dance to. I hope this song sings forever.

THE POEMS

Only in America

White privilege can save you
where God can't
Only in America

Ya brethren ain't ya brethren no more
They say heaven ain't Heaven no more

We cling to clouds, we roll up on shores
Roll up, and realize, heaven ain't Heaven no more

Children run around cold visiting rooms
waiting to see daddy who fell victim
to the 13th Amendment
Hour visits feel like 5 minutes.

We wanna be just like our daddies
Mass Incarceration is a bully
shaking a blind bum for his change
leaving him broker than before

No matter how hard you try,
you can't cage Luke Cage
forever
That's beauty

i pray, feet nailed to the floor
If you look hard enough, it's beauty
in the struggle
Maybe it's better here because i heard that
heaven ain't Heaven no more.

Joy and Anger

Timidness awards you two
Black eyes
Ever wonder why I'm the
"angry Black guy"

Confidence awards you,
you
Your flesh might burn
Your blood might churn
But…you'll be what everyone
else wants, which is,
to be themselves

Slouches can't survive monsoons
You have to be hotter than fire
or stronger than water, where
i come from

Die a coward or get crowned
Your crown might have thorns
but boy,
The JOY of being a King.

They Call Us CRAZY!

You have to be strong, because if you're weak,
you're gone.
We built this country,
they call us lazy
We resist oppression,
they call us CRAZY!
Nah
We're just livin in the U.S. baby
We gon fight
We gon win
We gon war
Again and again

Black. Blood. Drips.

Black. blood. drips.
on the concrete
Staining generations
That one lone sneaker
loses its foot when
bullets whack domes

For ages we've dodged hammers like wack-a-mole
Holy garments that weren't designed by Kanye
Bloody dread locs that weren't fabricated by Marc Jacobs,
If Heaven was a mile away, our legs would've been cut off
If we found the strength to journey, arriving at the pearly gates
On our hands and knees, just to see broken trees,
Black bosoms trembling, with black babies hanging from em

Having nightmares wondering
were you one of em?
Having nightmares wondering
were we one of em?
Having nightmares wondering
was i one of em?

Black.
Blood.
Drips.

Where is paradise for us?
Should we treasure harvest on the other side?
Is our treasure not here?
Do we love the mud because of the harvest is has,
Although our harvest has died?

Would you rather cook your own dinner?
Or
Would you rather eat the crumbs that
fall from the master's table?

Paradise

Dope

Gil Scott flows through my veins
Heroin flows through our parents

Dope is dope
We all are addicts

94

Ask Yourself

Strong
Black
Lionhearted
Liberated
Speak your mind
Then
Bullets fly at your cerebellum
Ask Malcolm
Ask Martin
Ask Pac
Ask Korryn
Ask Yourself
Is freedom worth dying for?
You're damn right

Acknowledgements

Picking up and reading *Raw Wounds* was not an obligation for you, and it means the world to me that you did. You could be anywhere else in the world, but you are here, with me. It brings me great joy when people read and listen to my work. Every line that I pen is much bigger than me, and I appreciate everyone who embraces Kondwani Fidel as a person and as an artist.

The night of February 10, 2013, at Virginia State University, I shared my poetry for the first time, and I want to thank everyone who has believed in me since then. Thank you, Professor Arnold Westbrook, for sparking my interest in becoming a reader and writer, my freshman year at Virginia State University. Also, thanks for being a conduit to my membership in The Omega Psi Phi Fraternity, Incorporated.

Thanks to Reginald Thomas II, D. Watkins, and Tariq Touré for your insight and mentorship during the development of *Raw Wounds*. So glad that we had the opportunity to "build."

I want to thank Mikea Hugley, not only for designing *Raw Wounds*, but also for being a good friend, who is now a part of my life forever. Also, thank you again Mikea, for putting up with my indecisiveness during the entire process of creating this book. This world needs your art in it, so don't ever stop creating magic.

Thank you, Kerry Graham, for the long nights of idea bouncing, planning, preparing, and copyediting that you did for *Raw Wounds*. Thank you, Kerry, for being the best manager that anyone could ask for. Not only do you support my art, but you help make me a better person and writer, due to your love for writing, living, and the progression of the youth in Baltimore City.

I want to thank both of my grandmothers for the sacrifices that you made to create a better life for me. You two are the reason why I have an enduring love and respect for all women, especially Black women persevering through the struggle.

Thanks to any and everybody who has inspired me in any form or fashion—through art or conversation. You also play a major role in the making of Kondwani Fidel.

Last but not least, I want to thank God for giving me an opportunity to leave footprints on his earth.

No matter what obstacles you face in life, always pursue your passion.

KONDWANI

FIDEL

Kondwani Fidel is a writer, speaker, and spoken word poet who holds a B.A. in English from Virginia State University. His work has been featured on The Root, Business Insider, Huffington Post, and elsewhere. He has lectured and shared poetry at countless universities, conferences, and literary events throughout the country.

He has a vast commitment to empowering people, in particularly, the youth, through literacy. He is from, and currently lives in, Baltimore, Maryland.

www.KondwaniFidel.com
Instagram, Twitter, Snapchat: @KondwaniFidel
Facebook: www.facebook.com/KondwaniFidel
Email: BookingKondwanifidel@gmail.com

Made in the USA
Middletown, DE
26 March 2017